DISABILITIES CAN'T STOP US!

# MICHAEL J. FOX
## Live in the Moment

Jeremy P. Morlock

**PowerKiDS press**

New York

Published in 2021 by The Rosen Publishing Group, Inc.
29 East 21st Street, New York, NY 10010

Copyright © 2021 by The Rosen Publishing Group, Inc.

All rights reserved. No part of this book may be reproduced in any form without permission in writing from the publisher, except by a reviewer.

First Edition

Editor: Elizabeth Krajnik
Book Design: Reann Nye

Photo Credits: Series art (background) Ratana21/Shutterstock.com; cover Cindy Ord/Getty Images Entertainment/Getty Images; p. 5 Theo Wargo/Getty Images Entertainment/Getty Images; p. 7 CBS Photo Archive/CBS/Getty Images; p. 9 Wally Fong/AP Images; p. 11 Universal Pictures/Moviepix/Getty Images; p. 13 Archive Photos/Moviepix/Getty Images; p. 15 Ron Galella/Ron Galella Collection/Getty Images; p. 17 Ron Galella, Ltd./Ron Galella Collection/Getty Images; p. 19 PAUL J. RICHARDS/AFP/Getty Images; p. 21 Evan Agostini/Getty Images Entertainment/Getty Images; pp. 23, 29 Jim Spellman/WireImage/Getty Images; p. 25 Scott Olson/ Getty Images News/Getty Images; p. 27 Jason LaVeris/FilmMagic/Getty Images; p. 28 David Livingston/ Getty Images Entertainment/Getty Images.

Library of Congress Cataloging-in-Publication Data

Names: Morlock, Jeremy (Jeremy P.), author.
Title: Live in the moment : Michael J. Fox / Jeremy P, Morlock.
Description: New York : PowerKids Press, [2021] | Series: Disabilities
  can't stop us! | Includes bibliographical references and index. |
  Summary: "Michael J. Fox found success as a film and television actor at
  an early age. However, when he was diagnosed with Parkinson's disease,
  his life and goals changed forever. Fox has continued acting, faced
  physical and emotional challenges, and shared his experiences and
  optimism with others. His foundation has raised more than $800 million
  to fund research to find a cure for Parkinson's disease. This book will
  show young readers more about Fox's life and views and help them
  understand the many issues people with disabilities face today"–
  Provided by publisher.
Identifiers: LCCN 2019027759 | ISBN 9781725311206 (library binding) | ISBN
  9781725311183 (paperback) | ISBN 9781725311190 | ISBN 9781725311190
  (6 pack)
Subjects: LCSH: Fox, Michael J., 1961–Juvenile literature. |
  Actors–United States–Biography–Juvenile literature. | Parkinson's
  disease–Patients–United States–Biography–Juvenile literature.
Classification: LCC PN2308.F69 M67 2021 | DDC 791.4302/8/092 [B]–dc23
LC record available at https://lccn.loc.gov/2019027759

Manufactured in the United States of America

CPSIA Compliance Information: Batch #CSPK20. For Further Information contact Rosen Publishing, New York, New York at 1-800-237-9932.

# CONTENTS

More than a Star .................................. 4
A Young Actor ..................................... 6
Life in Los Angeles ................................ 8
From TV to Movies ................................10
A Shaking Finger ..................................12
Keeping a Secret ..................................14
Telling the World .................................16
Parkinson's Disease Advocacy ...............18
Lucky Man ...........................................20
Looking for a Cure ...............................22
Getting Political ...................................24
Live in the Moment ............................. 26
Each Step Is a New Adventure ..............28
Timeline ..............................................30
Glossary ..............................................31
Index ...................................................32
Websites .............................................32

# More than a Star

When Michael J. Fox was **diagnosed** with young-onset Parkinson's disease in 1991, he was already a famous movie and TV actor. He was just 29 years old, and the diagnosis scared him. His doctor told him he only had 10 years left to work as an actor. Despite what the doctor said, Fox has continued to act in movies and on TV for more than 20 years.

Fox kept his diagnosis a secret until 1998, when he publicly announced he has Parkinson's disease. It was a huge news story. Fox realized he could use his platform as an actor to increase awareness of Parkinson's disease. In 2000, Fox created the Michael J. Fox **Foundation** for Parkinson's **Research** to raise money for research and to improve Parkinson's therapies, or treatments.

> On September 25, 2013, Michael J. Fox was a guest on *Late Night with Jimmy Fallon*. They talked about Fox's new show, *The Michael J. Fox Show*.

## Parkinson's Disease

Parkinson's disease is a **progressive** nervous system **disorder**. It affects how people move and, later, think. Parkinson's disease happens when nerve cells in the brain called neurons break down or die. This can cause **tremors**, slow movement, stiff muscles, problems with posture and balance, trouble blinking or smiling, trouble speaking, and trouble writing. Why people get Parkinson's disease is unknown. Even though there isn't a cure for Parkinson's disease yet, some medicines can improve symptoms, or the signs that show someone is sick. Some doctors also recommend surgery to improve symptoms.

# A Young Actor

Fox was born Michael Andrew Fox on June 9, 1961, in Edmonton, Alberta, Canada, to William and Phyllis Fox. His father was in the Canadian armed forces and his job required the family to move around a lot. In 1971, the Foxes finally settled near Vancouver, British Columbia.

Fox got his first **professional** acting job when he was 16 years old. He landed the part of a 12-year-old named Jamie on the Canadian Broadcasting Corporation (CBC) **sitcom** *Leo and Me*. Shortly after, Fox got the lead role in a TV film. Fox continued acting during high school, but he eventually dropped out to pursue acting full time. In April 1979, when Fox was just shy of 18 years old, he moved to Los Angeles, California, for more job opportunities.

> One of Fox's first recurring, or returning, roles in Hollywood was as Willy-Joe Hall in the TV drama series *Palmerstown, U.S.A.*

# Life in Los Angeles

Fox's early years in Los Angeles were hard. For the first two-and-a-half years there, Fox got steady acting jobs. But by the third year, he barely had enough money to buy food. He didn't care to keep track of how much money he was making and how much he was spending.

Then, Fox started to work harder to get more acting jobs. Although he didn't have much money, he put more thought into how he looked and the **auditions** he was going to. His luck changed in 1982 when he was cast as a high school student named Alex P. Keaton on the TV comedy *Family Ties*. People in Hollywood began noticing Fox's comedic talent and leading man qualities.

*Family Ties* made Fox famous. It aired from 1982 to 1989.

# From TV to Movies

Fox's role on *Family Ties* opened up the possibilities for him to get more acting jobs in Hollywood. In 1985, Fox was cast as Marty McFly, a time-traveling teenager, in *Back to the Future*. This happened in part because Steven Spielberg, the film's executive producer, was good friends with Gary David Goldberg, the creator of *Family Ties*. Fox replaced another actor who'd already been filming the part of McFly. For three months, Fox filmed *Family Ties* and *Back to the Future* at the same time.

*Back to the Future* was a box office hit. At just 24 years old, Fox was a Hollywood star. In 1988, Fox married Tracy Pollan, who played Alex P. Keaton's girlfriend on *Family Ties*. Their first child, Sam, was born in 1989.

> **UNSTOPPABLE!**
> Fox won three Emmy awards in 1986, 1987, and 1988 and one Golden Globe award in 1989 for his role in *Family Ties*.

In *Back to the Future*, Marty McFly travels from 1985 to 1955, the year his parents started dating in high school.

# A Shaking Finger

On the morning of November 13, 1990, Fox woke up and noticed his left pinky finger had a tremor. No matter what he did, his pinky wouldn't stop wiggling. He thought the tremor—and what he would later learn were other symptoms of Parkinson's disease—was the result of an injury. For about a year, he saw different doctors who weren't sure what the problem was.

In September 1991, Fox was diagnosed with young-onset Parkinson's disease. Fox was only 29 years old. The doctor said he might have been living with the disease for as many as 10 years without knowing it. The diagnosis was surprising to Fox and the doctors. His finger was just the start. Over time, his symptoms would worsen.

Fox was busy filming *Doc Hollywood* when he experienced the first symptoms of Parkinson's disease.

## Young-Onset Parkinson's Disease

Young-onset Parkinson's disease (YOPD) is when people younger than 50 years old are diagnosed with the disease. About 1 million people in the United States have Parkinson's disease, and between 2 to 10 percent of those people have YOPD. It often takes people with YOPD a long time to be given a proper diagnosis. YOPD presents younger people with a different set of challenges. Many may still be working and might not have enough time to receive the care they need. They may have children who need their attention or they may want to start a family.

# Keeping a Secret

Fox told only his family he'd been diagnosed with Parkinson's disease. He took medicine for his Parkinson's symptoms and **abused** alcohol to deal with his feelings and have a sense of control. However, this wasn't helping him. Fox decided to get sober, or stop drinking, and accept that he didn't have control over his body. He sought therapy to help make sense of his diagnosis and emotions.

Fox realized that even though he couldn't choose to not have Parkinson's disease, he could choose to learn more about the disease and how it would change his life. He chose to make better choices for his treatment, chose to grow his family and strengthen his friendships, and chose only to work jobs in New York, where his family was based.

## UNSTOPPABLE!

In March 1998, Fox had brain surgery to ease some of his Parkinson's disease symptoms. The surgery almost completely stopped the constant shaking of his left arm. But the results of the surgery were only temporary.

Fox convinced Gary David Goldberg to produce *Spin City* in New York City instead of Los Angeles so Fox could be close to his family.

# Telling the World

In an interview with *People* magazine in December 1998, Fox announced he'd been diagnosed with Parkinson's disease. His story made headlines. National TV programs interviewed Fox. Newspapers and magazines printed stories about him and information about Parkinson's disease. After telling the world, Fox felt a sense of relief.

Many people wrote to Fox, telling him about their experiences with Parkinson's disease. "When I did share my story the response was overwhelming, humbling, and deeply inspiring," he said. He realized that, as a famous person, he had the power to help people with Parkinson's disease. "What celebrity has given me is the opportunity to raise the visibility of Parkinson's disease and focus attention on the desperate need for more research dollars," he said.

> In 1999, Fox was the winner of *GQ* magazine's Men of the Year award for television comedy.

## Quality of Life

In Fox's announcement, he talked about how everyone who has Parkinson's disease meets the same end. "The end of the story is you die. We all die. So, accepting that, the issue becomes one of quality of life." Even though people with Parkinson's disease often can't do the things they used to, they can still find a way to lead happy and fulfilling lives. After his diagnosis, Fox can't play hockey anymore. Instead, he chooses to do other enjoyable activities that don't make his symptoms worse.

# Parkinson's Disease Advocacy

In 1999, Joan Samuelson, the founder and director of the Parkinson's Action Network, approached Fox to be part of a panel of people who'd speak to members of Congress about giving money to the National Institute of Neurological Disorders and Stroke. On September 28, 1999, Fox spoke out in his first act of public **advocacy**.

In Fox's **testimony** to Congress, he explained what it's like living with Parkinson's disease, the effects that medicines and therapies have on people with the disease, and how people could benefit from more funding for Parkinson's disease research.

After speaking to Congress, Fox and other people on the panel spoke more closely with individual members of Congress. Members of the House of Representatives promised to work on increasing funding for Parkinson's disease research.

## UNSTOPPABLE!

In 1984, Muhammad Ali, one of the greatest boxers in the world, was diagnosed with Parkinson's disease. Like Fox, Ali used his celebrity status to raise public awareness of the disease.

One of Fox's most famous lines in his testimony to Congress was, "In my 40s, I can expect challenges most people wouldn't face until their 70s and 80s, if ever. But with your help, if we all do everything we can to [get rid of] this disease, when I'm in my 50s I'll be dancing at my children's weddings."

## The History of Parkinson's Disease

Parkinson's disease has had a number of names throughout history. However, British physician James Parkinson was the first to describe the disease in 1817 in his "Essay on the Shaking Palsy." Parkinson's disease is a type of Parkinsonism, which refers to diseases with symptoms similar to Parkinson's disease. However, Parkinson's disease is set apart from other types of Parkinsonism because it has no known cause. Jean-Martin Charcot further researched Parkinson's disease and other types of Parkinsonism and informed people around the world about these diseases.

# Lucky Man

On January 18, 2000, Fox announced that he'd be leaving *Spin City* at the end of the show's fourth season to spend more time with his family. He wanted to leave before his Parkinson's disease made it impossible for him to work. Even though Fox chose to leave *Spin City*, he assured the public that he wasn't quitting acting, producing, or directing.

Fox also wanted to spend more time working toward finding a cure for Parkinson's disease. Later in 2000, Fox launched the Michael J. Fox Foundation for Parkinson's Research. The foundation's mission is to find a cure for Parkinson's disease through research and improving therapies and treatments for people with Parkinson's disease. Since it was founded, the Michael J. Fox Foundation has raised over $800 million to fund Parkinson's disease research programs.

## UNSTOPPABLE!

The proceeds of Fox's 2002 **memoir** *Lucky Man* went to the Michael J. Fox Foundation for Parkinson's Research. The book was a *New York Times* bestseller.

On November 11, 2006, Muhammad Ali, right, attended the A Funny Thing Happened on the Way to Cure Parkinson's event, which raised money for the Michael J. Fox Foundation for Parkinson's Research.

## Working with Parkinson's Disease

The symptoms of Parkinson's disease can make it very hard for people to keep working. However, because Parkinson's disease affects everyone differently, not everyone will feel the need to tell those at their workplace. The Americans with Disabilities Act enforces people with disabilities' right to reasonable accommodations in their workplace if they have told their employer and have filled out a request. Keeping a job means people with Parkinson's disease are able to keep their health insurance and continue paying for treatments and medications.

# Looking for a Cure

The Michael J. Fox Foundation for Parkinson's Research pays for programs to help find a cure for Parkinson's disease. About 30 percent of the funds the foundation raises go to research teams outside the United States. The foundation does this so new developments can be shared quickly and in as many places as possible.

To find a cure, the Michael J. Fox Foundation for Parkinson's Research focuses on finding out more about Parkinson's disease on a biological level. How does it come about? How does it progress? How can it be treated over time? It also focuses on how patients can receive therapies tailored to their specific symptoms. For this to happen, the foundation has a strong team of researchers, patients to participate in studies and trials, and donors.

Other famous people, such as journalist Katie Couric, center, and her husband, John Molner, left, also help bring awareness to and raise money for Parkinson's disease research.

# Getting Political

Fox played characters involved in politics on *Spin City* and in the movie *The American President*. Since launching the Michael J. Fox Foundation for Parkinson's Disease, Fox has become more involved in politics in real life.

In the early years of Parkinson's disease research, many scientists believed that **embryonic stem cells** could cure a number of conditions. Stem cell research often divides people politically. Some people feel that stem cell research isn't right, while others feel it's very important. Fox spoke in favor of stem cell research. He also supported politicians who wanted more stem cell research.

In 2012, however, Fox announced that the Michael J. Fox Foundation for Parkinson's Research would focus on other types of research that are more promising.

## UNSTOPPABLE!

On *The Good Wife*, Fox played Louis Canning, a character with a disability similar to Parkinson's disease. Fox wanted to show that people with disabilities have all types of personalities and that you shouldn't feel bad for them just because they have a disability.

Fox supported Tammy Duckworth in her run for a seat in Congress. Duckworth was in favor of stem cell research.

# Live in the Moment

Family is the most important thing to Fox. Even though the first few years following his Parkinson's diagnosis were hard on Fox and his family, he's said that accepting that he has Parkinson's disease has allowed him to be a better husband to Tracy and father to his son and two daughters. Fox has learned to appreciate his life as it is. "Live in the moment, enjoy the day, make the most of what you have," he said.

Since Fox was diagnosed, he's made many choices on how to live his life. "The only unavailable choice was whether or not to have Parkinson's. Everything else was up to me," he wrote in his second memoir, *Always Looking Up: The Adventures of an Incurable Optimist*.

### UNSTOPPABLE!

In 2013, Fox decided to go back to full-time TV acting. He played the role of Mike Henry in a comedy inspired by Fox's life and called *The Michael J. Fox Show*.

On February 26, 2017, Michael J. Fox and Seth Rogen presented the award for Best Film Editing at the Academy Awards.

# Each Step Is a New Adventure

Medication and other therapies have helped Fox control his Parkinson's disease symptoms over the years. However, he's spoken about how other people have a much harder time controlling their symptoms, coming to terms emotionally with having a progressive disease, and continuing to live their lives as normally as they can.

## UNSTOPPABLE!

*Always Looking Up: The Adventures of an Incurable Optimist* was published in 2009. It debuted at No. 2 on the *New York Times* bestseller list. It also had a TV special that was nominated for an Emmy for Outstanding Nonfiction Special.

Michael J. Fox has said that family is more than just an important part of life—it's everything. Here, he is pictured with his wife, Tracy, and his children, from left to right, Schuyler Frances, Aquinnah Kathleen, Sam Michael, and Esmé Annabelle.

In 2018, Fox had spinal surgery. He was in a wheelchair and needed to learn how to walk again. The experience taught him another lesson. "I realized I have to take everything one step at a time so I don't fall down," Fox said. "You have more time that way. Each step is a new adventure." Fox's positive outlook keeps him hopeful that one day there will be a cure for Parkinson's disease.

# TIMELINE

**June 9, 1961**
Fox is born as Michael Andrew Fox in Edmonton, Alberta, Canada, to William and Phyllis Fox.

**1971**
The Fox family settles outside Vancouver, British Columbia, Canada.

**1976**
Fox is hired to act on the Canadian TV sitcom *Leo and Me*.

**1979**
Fox moves to Los Angeles, California, to find more work as an actor.

**1982**
*Family Ties* becomes a hit show, making Fox famous.

**1988**
Fox marries Tracy Pollan, a former costar from *Family Ties*.

**1989**
Fox's son, Samuel, is born.

**1991**
Fox is diagnosed with young-onset Parkinson's disease.

**1995**
Fox's twin daughters, Aquinnah and Schuyler, are born.

**1998**
In an interview with *People* magazine, Fox reveals that he has Parkinson's disease.

**1999**
Fox asks the U.S. Congress to spend more on Parkinson's disease research.

**2000**
Fox creates the Michael J. Fox Foundation for Parkinson's Research.

**2001**
Fox's daughter Esmé is born.

**2010**
Fox begins a recurring role as a character with a disability on *The Good Wife*.

**2013**
Fox returns to TV full time in *The Michael J. Fox Show*.

**2018**
Fox recovers from a spinal problem not caused by his Parkinson's disease.

# GLOSSARY

**abuse:** To use improperly or in harmful amounts.

**advocacy:** The act or process of supporting a cause.

**audition:** A short performance to test the talents of someone such as a dancer, singer, or actor.

**diagnose:** To recognize a disease by its signs and symptoms.

**disorder:** A physical or mental condition that isn't normal or healthy.

**embryonic stem cell:** Cells that come from embryos, which are unborn human beings in the earliest stages of growth when their basic structures are being formed.

**foundation:** An organization that is created and supported with money that people give in order to do something that helps society.

**memoir:** A written account in which someone talks about past experiences.

**professional:** Having to do with a job someone does for a living.

**progressive:** Taking place gradually or step by step.

**research:** Careful study that is done to find and report new knowledge about something.

**sitcom:** A TV show about a group of characters who are involved in different funny situations.

**testimony:** Proof or evidence that something exists or is true.

**tremor:** A trembling or shaking especially from weakness or disease.

# INDEX

**A**
*Alberta*, 6, 30
Ali, Muhammad, 18, 21
*Always Looking Up: The Adventures of an Incurable Optimist*, 26, 28
*American President, The*, 24

**B**
*Back to the Future*, 10, 11
British Columbia, 6, 30

**C**
California, 6, 30
Canada, 6, 30
Congress, U.S., 18, 19, 25, 30

**D**
*Doc Hollywood*, 12
Duckworth, Tammy, 25

**E**
Edmonton, 6, 30
Emmy awards, 10, 28

**F**
*Family Ties*, 8, 10, 30
Fox, Phyllis, 6, 30
Fox, William, 6, 30

**G**
Goldberg, Gary David, 10, 15
Golden Globe, 10
*Good Wife, The*, 24, 30

**L**
*Leo and Me*, 6, 30
Los Angeles, 6, 8, 15, 30
*Lucky Man*, 20

**M**
Michael J. Fox Foundation for Parkinson's Research, 4, 20, 21, 22, 24, 30
*Michael J. Fox Show, The*, 4, 26, 30

**N**
New York City, 14, 15

**P**
*Palmerstown, U.S.A.*, 6
Parkinson's Action Network, 18
Parkinson's disease, 4, 5, 12, 13, 14, 16, 17, 18, 19, 20, 21, 22, 24, 26, 28, 29, 30
Pollan, Tracy, 10, 26, 29, 30

**S**
Samuelson, Joan, 18
Spielberg, Steven, 10
*Spin City*, 15, 20, 24

**V**
Vancouver, 6, 30

**Y**
young-onset Parkinson's disease (YOPD), 12, 13, 30

# WEBSITES

Due to the changing nature of Internet links, PowerKids Press has developed an online list of websites related to the subject of this book. This site is updated regularly. Please use this link to access the list: www.powerkidslinks.com/dcsu/fox